EVERYTHING SPORTS

EVERYTHING FOOTBALL

CORBU STATHES

SportsZone

An Imprint of Abdo Publishing
abdobooks.com

abdobooks.com

Published by Abdo Publishing, a division of ABDO, PO Box 398166, Minneapolis, Minnesota 55439.

Printed in the United States of America, North Mankato, Minnesota.
052024
092024

THIS BOOK CONTAINS RECYCLED MATERIALS

Cover Photos: Nick Wosika/Icon Sportswire/Getty Images, front (Justin Jefferson); Aaron M. Sprecher/AP Images, front (Jalen Hurts); Shutterstock Images, front (background), back
Interior Photos: Sarin Images/Granger Historical Picture Archive, 4–5; Bob Stowell/Archive Photos/Getty Images, 6–7; NFL Photos/AP Images, 8–9; Bettmann/Getty Images, 10–11; Focus on Sport/Getty Images, 12–13, 14–15; Focus on Sport/Getty Images Sport/Getty Images, 16–17, 57; Perry Knotts/Getty Images Sport/Getty Images, 19; Todd Kirkland/Getty Images Sport/Getty Images, 20–21; Keith Gillett/Icon Sportswire/Getty Images, 22–23; John Cordes/Icon Sportswire/Getty Images, 24–25; Hy Peskin Archive/Archive Photos/Getty Images, 26–27; Stephen Dunn/Allsport/Hulton Archive/Getty Images, 28; Andy Lyons/USFL/Getty Images Sport/Getty Images, 30–31; Steve Russell/Toronto Star/Getty Images, 32–33; Vic Stein/Getty Images Sport/Getty Images, 35; Fred Kfoury III/Icon Sportswire/Getty Images, 36–37; John E. Sokolowski/Getty Images Sport/Getty Images, 38–39; Arina P. Habich/Shutterstock Images, 40–41; Andy Lewis/Icon Sportswire/Getty Images, 42–43; Stan Grossfeld/Boston Globe/Getty Images, 44–45; James Nielsen/Houston Chronicle/Hearst Newspapers/Getty Images, 46–47; Brett Carlsen/Getty Images Sport/Getty Images, 49; George Gojkovich/Getty Images Sport/Getty Images, 50–51; Allen Kee/Getty Images Sport/Getty Images, 52–53; Jamie Squire/Getty Images Sport/Getty Images, 54–55; Al Behrman/AP Images, 58–59; Perry Knotts/AP Images, 61

Editor: Charlie Beattie
Series Designer: Karli Kruse

Library of Congress Control Number: 2023949387
Publisher's Cataloging-in-Publication Data
Names: Stathes, Corbu, author.
Title: Everything football / by Corbu Stathes
Description: Minneapolis, Minnesota: Abdo Publishing, 2025 | Series: Everything sports | Includes online resources and index.
Identifiers: ISBN 9781098293574 (lib. bdg.) | ISBN 9798384912842 (ebook)
Subjects: LCSH: Football--Juvenile literature. | American football--Juvenile literature. | Football teams--Juvenile literature. | Football players--Juvenile literature. | Football coaches--Juvenile literature. | Football stadiums--Juvenile literature. | Football managers--Juvenile literature. | Football fans--Juvenile literature. | Football--Records--Juvenile literature. | National Football League--Juvenile literature.
Classification: DDC 796.332--dc23

TABLE OF CONTENTS

CHAPTER ONE

AN EVOLVING GAME

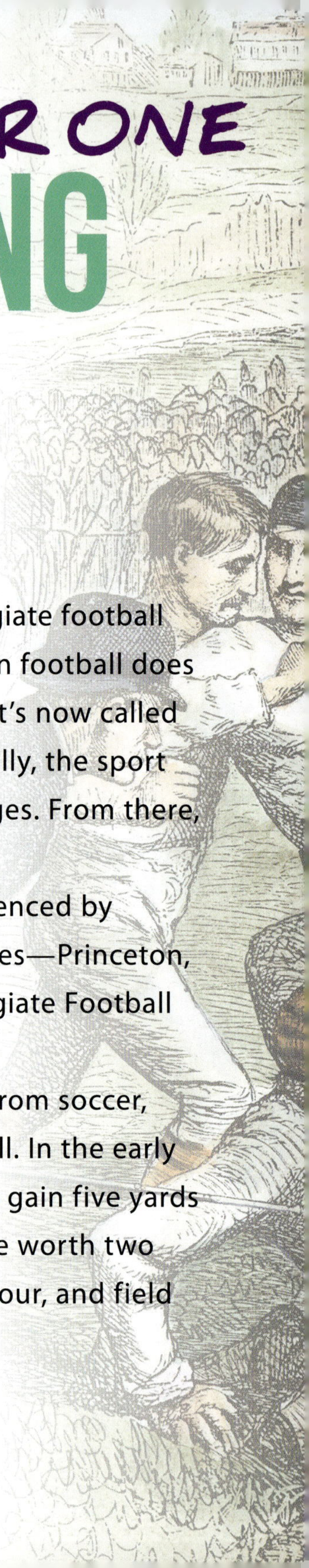

Rutgers and Princeton played the first collegiate football game in 1869. It looked much different than football does today. The game more closely resembled what's now called soccer. Players mostly used their feet. Eventually, the sport became popular with the major eastern colleges. From there, football began to evolve into today's version.

The game's development was largely influenced by three universities in the northeast United States—Princeton, Yale, and Rutgers. They created the Intercollegiate Football Association to devise a set of rules.

Even after changes made football unique from soccer, the sport still looked little like modern football. In the early days, a team had three plays, called downs, to gain five yards in order to keep possession. Touchdowns were worth two points. The goal after touchdown was worth four, and field goals were worth five.

An artist's print shows an 1879 college football game between Yale and Princeton.

New England Patriots running back Curtis Martin, *left*, tries to break a tackle during a game in 1995.

Goal posts were located on the goal line rather than at the back of the end zone. Coaches also played, and only a certain number of players could be substituted at a time. Most players also played on both sides of the ball. Players who specialized on only offense or defense weren't common until decades later. And the forward pass didn't become legal until 1906.

The game of football continues to evolve. But the excitement of the fans in the stands remains constant. The most dedicated supporters plan their weekends around high school, college, and National Football League (NFL) games. Without a doubt, football is America's most popular sport.

THE FATHER OF FOOTBALL

Walter Camp became a member of the Intercollegiate Football Association rules committee in 1878. At the time, he was still a student at Yale University. He spent the next 48 years on the committee while also playing and coaching. In that time, he oversaw many important changes to the game. The 11-player team, quarterbacks calling signals, and even the line of scrimmage were all Camp's ideas. Camp also wrote the first book on football. And he was one of the first to use pictures and illustrations as coaching aids.

CHAPTER TWO

PRO FOOTBALL REIGNS

In the early days, college football was king. But it was only a matter of time before professional leagues developed. Early attempts to form leagues in Pennsylvania and Ohio fell apart for a variety of reasons. The idea of signing players to contracts to stay with one team was still unheard of. Players jumped from team to team, chasing the highest offers. Bidding wars arose for the best players. That caused money problems for some teams. Professional teams also fielded college players while they were still in school.

Team owners knew they needed to create a set of rules that all teams would follow. So in 1920, they came together to form the American Professional Football Association. The new league featured teams in Illinois, Indiana, Michigan, New York, and Ohio. They all agreed to play by the same rules. By 1922, the league had 18 teams. It also changed its name to the National Football League.

Professional football began in the 1890s, roughly 30 years before the NFL was created.

The college game was still much more popular with fans. But in 1925, that began to change. Red Grange, one of the biggest names in college football, signed with the Chicago Bears. The former University of Illinois halfback led the Bears on a two-month tour of the Midwest and East Coast. In that time, the Bears played 19 games. Hundreds of thousands of fans came out to watch Grange and his teammates. Historians say this tour helped make professional football legitimate.

CARDINAL LEGACY

In 1899, building contractor Chris O'Brien formed a team in his Chicago neighborhood. That team still exists as the Arizona Cardinals. It's the oldest active team in the league. The team went by different names early on. In 1901, O'Brien bought a set of used uniforms from the University of Chicago. They were dark red, so the team became known as the Cardinals. The name stuck as the team played in Chicago, then St. Louis, and now Arizona.

The NFL was already the country's main professional football league. But it wasn't as big a deal as it is today. Early on, other upstart leagues tried to challenge the NFL. None lasted long. But one challenger had a lasting impact on football. The American Football League (AFL) began play in 1960. Lamar Hunt and Bud Adams had wanted to own NFL teams, but the league turned them down. Instead, they

Sportswriters dubbed Red Grange the "Galloping Ghost" for his smooth running style.

Ten NFL teams, including the New England Patriots (in red) and Kansas City Chiefs (in white), started in the AFL.

gathered six other owners and started their own league. The AFL embraced a wide-open passing game. It was the opposite of the defensive, grinding style of football in the NFL. The AFL also drew fan interest by outspending the NFL to sign some big-name players.

AFL and NFL teams soon began fighting to sign the best talent. Instead of trying to compete, the leagues eventually agreed to merge. The process began with the 1966 NFL and AFL champions meeting in what later became known as the first Super Bowl. In 1970, all 10 AFL teams joined the NFL. They combined with three NFL teams to form the new American Football Conference (AFC). The other 13 NFL teams made up the National Football Conference (NFC).

Today, the NFL has 32 teams. Each conference consists of four divisions with four teams each. Seven teams from each conference reach the playoffs. And every year, the AFC and NFC champions still meet in the Super Bowl to determine the NFL championship.

CHAPTER THREE
SUPER BOWL SUNDAY

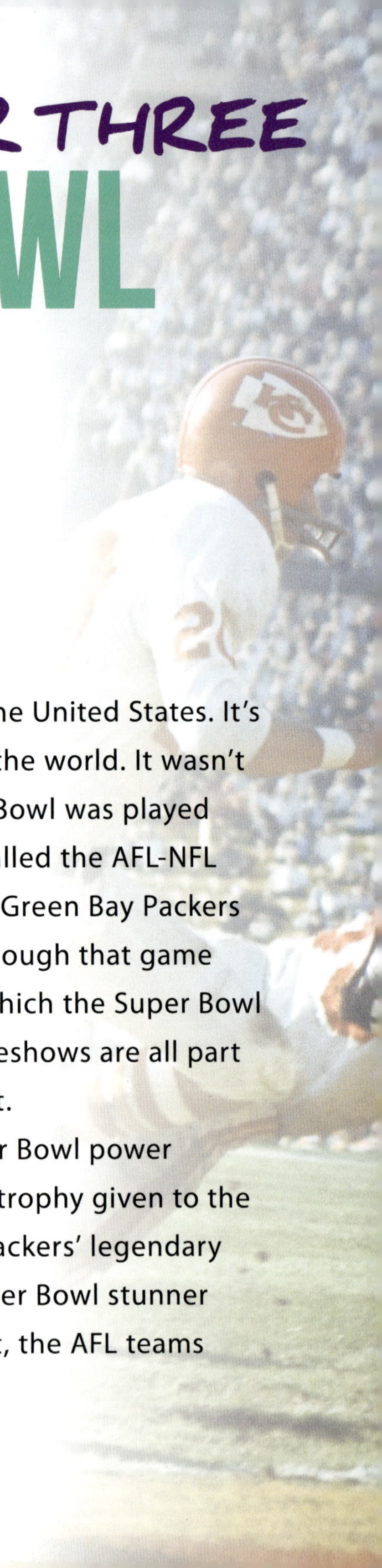

The Super Bowl isn't just a big deal in the United States. It's one of the biggest sporting events in the world. It wasn't always that way, though. The first Super Bowl was played on January 15, 1967. At the time, it was called the AFL-NFL Championship Game. The NFL champion Green Bay Packers beat AFL champion Kansas City 35–10. Though that game didn't sell out, it set a foundation from which the Super Bowl grew. Great dynasties, traditions, and sideshows are all part of what makes the game such a big event.

Green Bay proved to be the first Super Bowl power when it won the next year, too. Now the trophy given to the Super Bowl winners is named after the Packers' legendary coach, Vince Lombardi. The first true Super Bowl stunner came after the 1968 season. At that point, the AFL teams

Green Bay Packers running back Elijah Pitts (22) scores a touchdown late in the third quarter of the first Super Bowl.

had looked inferior to their NFL opponents. Then, in Super Bowl III, quarterback Joe Namath and the AFL's New York Jets shocked the world by beating the NFL's Baltimore Colts 16–7. That was also the first time the game was officially called the Super Bowl.

The Super Bowl is played in a different calendar year than the regular season. This created a potential for confusion when naming the game. The solution was to use Roman numerals. The fifth Super Bowl, played on January 17, 1971, was the first game to use them. It was known as Super Bowl V.

TROPHY CABINETS

The New England Patriots and the Pittsburgh Steelers share the record with six Super Bowl wins. The Patriots made nine appearances spanning the 2001 and 2018 seasons. Tom Brady started at quarterback for all six wins. He also won a Super Bowl with the Tampa Bay Buccaneers after leaving New England. Brady's seven Super Bowl wins are more than any other player. In fact, no NFL team can match Brady's mark.

The Super Bowl is held in a different location every year. It's usually played in a city with warm weather. Miami hosted 11 of the first 57 Super Bowls, followed by New Orleans with 10 and Los Angeles with seven. Still, some cold-weather cities have hosted, too. Super Bowl LII was played in February 2018 in Minneapolis.

New York Jets quarterback Joe Namath famously predicted his team would beat the Baltimore Colts before Super Bowl III.

The temperature outside was negative nine degrees Fahrenheit (–23°C). That made it the coldest Super Bowl day ever. Luckily for fans, the game was played inside US Bank Stadium. No one was uncomfortable watching the Philadelphia Eagles defeat the New England Patriots 41–33.

The Super Bowl always draws the largest TV audience of the year in the United States. In fact, many of the most-watched shows of all time are Super Bowls. Some of the fans tuning in at home aren't just watching for the game. The Super Bowl halftime show has drawn some of the biggest names in music to perform. Among those who have headlined the halftime show are Michael Jackson, Prince, Beyoncé, and Rihanna. The Super Bowl is also the biggest day of the year for TV advertisements.

With such a big audience, companies pay huge amounts of money to run commercials during the game. Many of these commercials are aired for the first time at the game. They have developed a reputation as being clever and memorable advertisements. It's all part of the spectacle that makes the Super Bowl an American tradition.

Kansas City Chiefs quarterback Patrick Mahomes hoists the Vince Lombardi Trophy after Kansas City defeated the San Francisco 49ers in Super Bowl LVIII in February 2024.

CHAPTER FOUR

COLLEGE FOOTBALL SATURDAYS

The game of football was born on college campuses, and college football remains a huge draw. Some college stadiums hold more than 100,000 fans. Many of these fans went to the school they root for, or grew up in the area. They often hold deep grudges against their school's rivals, too. Those attachments and feelings make college games electric affairs.

The National Collegiate Athletic Association (NCAA) is the largest governing body of college sports. In football, the NCAA has three levels. Division III consists of the smallest schools. Division II is the next step up. And Division I includes the biggest colleges and universities in the country.

University of Alabama quarterback Jalen Milroe takes on two University of Georgia defenders during the 2023 Southeastern Conference Championship Game.

THE HEISMAN TROPHY

The Heisman Trophy is awarded to the top college football player each year. Jay Berwanger, a running back from the University of Chicago, became the first winner in 1935. Ohio State tailback Archie Griffin is the only back-to-back winner, having won in 1974 and 1975. Charles Woodson, a defensive back from the University of Michigan, became the first defensive player to win the Heisman in 1997.

Division I football is divided into two tiers. The Football Bowl Subdivision (FBS) has the biggest programs. The NCAA FBS champion is determined by the College Football Playoff (CFP). The Football Championship Subdivision (FCS) teams play a 24-team tournament at the end of the season to determine a champion.

But the action on the field is only part of what draws fans to college football. Many fans enjoy the traditions typically tied to the game. Marching bands parade across campus and perform at halftime. At tailgate parties, fans share food, drinks, and stories of memorable games. College football fans often plan their whole weekends around the games. Many travel to watch their team on the road and make friends with fellow fans.

Of course, every school has at least one team its fans especially love to beat. Sometimes the schools are in the same state, such as Purdue and Indiana. Others might share

Student marching bands add to the spectacle of college football games each Saturday.

Some rivalries stretch across the country. Every year, Notre Dame and USC play for a traveling trophy called the Jeweled Shillelagh.

a border, as is the case with Georgia and Florida. Others are just a few miles apart, such as California and Stanford.

Rivalry games are the first ones fans circle on the calendar when a new season's schedule comes out. Some look forward to Ohio State against Michigan. Others want to see USC play UCLA, Oklahoma battle Texas, or Army vs. Navy. Most of the traditional matchups are played every year, as the teams often share a conference. And sometimes the winner takes home a traveling trophy. Minnesota and Wisconsin play for Paul Bunyan's Axe. The Fremont Cannon is on the line when Nevada faces the University of Nevada-Las Vegas. Mississippi State and Mississippi battle over the Golden Egg. The trophies stay on the winning teams' campuses until their rivals win them back.

At the end of the season, the CFP determines the FBS national championship. For years, polls of coaches and sportswriters voted on which team was No. 1. In the early 1990s, the push to decide the title on the field took form. From 1998 to 2013, the Bowl Championship Series determined the two best teams each season and matched them in a national title game. The CFP started in 2014 with the top four teams playing two semifinal games and a championship game. The field expanded to 12 teams in 2024.

CHAPTER FIVE

RIVAL LEAGUES

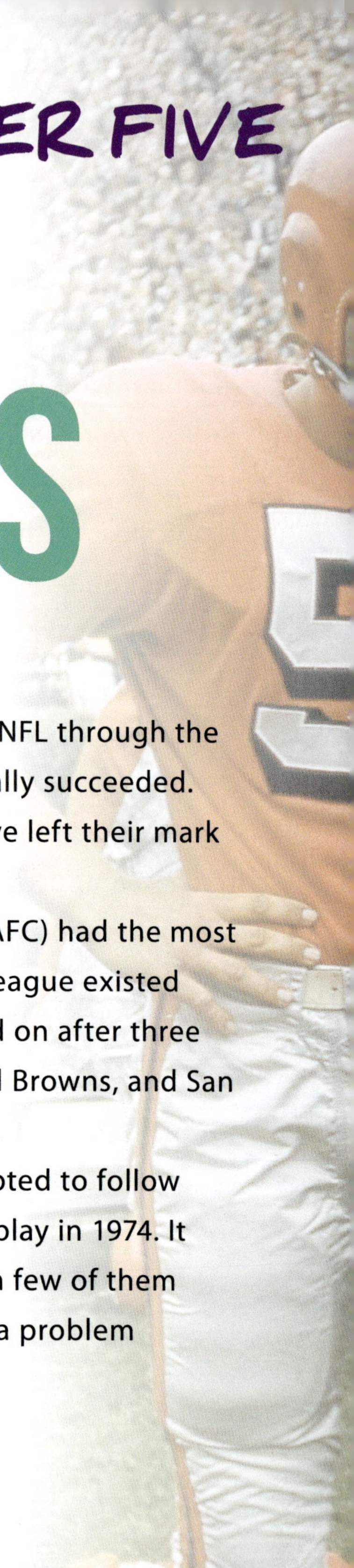

Other leagues have tried to challenge the NFL through the years. Only the AFL in the early 1960s really succeeded. However, other upstart football leagues have left their mark in other ways.

The All-America Football Conference (AAFC) had the most success of the NFL's early challengers. The league existed only from 1946 to 1949. But the league lived on after three of its teams—the Baltimore Colts, Cleveland Browns, and San Francisco 49ers—were admitted to the NFL.

The World Football League (WFL) attempted to follow the AFL's playbook. The new league began play in 1974. It tried to raid the NFL of its top players, and a few of them jumped to the new league. But money was a problem

The San Francisco 49ers spent four seasons in the AAFC before joining the NFL.

Hall of Fame quarterback Jim Kelly starred for the USFL's Houston Gamblers in the 1980s before moving to the NFL with the Buffalo Bills.

from the start. After a number of teams failed to pay their players, the WFL folded in the middle of its second season.

The United States Football League (USFL) was the next one to take on the NFL. The USFL's strategy was to play its games in the spring instead of fall. That meant fans could still invest time in their favorite NFL and college teams in the fall, then turn to the new league in the spring. It began play in March 1983 with 12 teams in cities from coast to coast.

The USFL convinced a handful of NFL veterans to get on board. But the league's bigger focus was trying to attract college stars to pick the new league over the NFL. In many ways, that strategy worked. Three consecutive Heisman Trophy winners signed with the USFL. Four more future Pro Football Hall of Famers began their professional careers in the USFL. The league had plenty of talent on the field. Because of that, many fans tuned in on TV.

After the 1985 season, a group of USFL owners wanted to challenge the NFL even more directly. They decided to move the 1986 season to the fall. The hope was to force another merger, similar to the one the AFL negotiated in the 1960s. But by the mid-1980s the NFL was better established. It had a

GOING CONTINENTAL

The NFL started a European league in 1991 that ran until 2007 under several different names. It started as the World League of American Football and was known as NFL Europa when it shut down in 2007. Some of the NFL's biggest names got their start in the league, including quarterback Kurt Warner and kicker Adam Vinatieri.

lot of money and even more patience. Instead of panicking, NFL owners waited for the USFL to fall apart, and it did. The USFL folded in 1986.

Other spring leagues tried to follow in the USFL's footsteps. The Xtreme Football League (XFL) debuted in 2001 with a promise of football that was more of a show like professional wrestling. That league lasted only one season. The league returned in 2020 without the wrestling personas and showed early signs of promise. However, it folded midseason due to the COVID-19 pandemic. Not to be deterred, the XFL returned again in 2023, this time with new ownership.

By then, the USFL had made a comeback as well. That league returned in the spring of 2022. Both the new USFL and XFL had a long way to go to truly challenge the NFL. But they had a plan. In 2023, the two leagues announced a merger to create one spring league going forward.

One league managed to stick around much longer. Having a wildly different format might have helped. The Arena Football League began play in the late 1980s. Teams played football on artificial turf inside basketball and hockey arenas. The smaller field and other rule changes created a fast paced, high-scoring game. At times, the league enjoyed a lot of fan support. However, the Arena League also had to

Running back C. J. Marable and the Birmingham Stallions defeated the Pittsburgh Maulers 28–12 in the 2023 USFL Championship Game.

Wide receiver Tyson Philpot of the CFL's Montreal Alouettes celebrates the winning touchdown in the 2023 Grey Cup.

cease operations for a year in 2009. It folded again in 2019, but league officials planned to bring it back again.

The Canadian Football League (CFL) also has some unique rules. But unlike some of the upstart leagues, the CFL proved to be much more than a gimmick. In fact, the league has been around since 1956, and it has been called the CFL since 1958. Further, the league champion wins the Grey Cup, which has been around since 1909. Today's CFL includes nine teams, from British Columbia in the west to Montreal in the east.

A handful of future NFL stars first showcased their talents in the CFL. Hall of Fame quarterback Warren Moon played for the Edmonton Eskimos from 1978 to 1983. He was the Most Valuable Player (MVP) of the Grey Cup twice. At 5 feet, 10 inches, quarterback Doug Flutie was thought to be too short for the NFL. Instead, he went to the CFL and won three Grey Cups in the 1990s. In 1998, he signed with the Buffalo Bills and played eight more NFL seasons.

Other players leave the NFL and become CFL legends. Mike Pringle played briefly for the NFL's Atlanta Falcons in 1990. In 1992, he left for the CFL. The running back retired in 2004 having set CFL records of 16,425 rushing yards and 127 touchdowns.

CHAPTER SIX

EQUIPMENT EVOLUTION

Helmets and shoulder pads create a distinctive look for football players. But they weren't always part of the game. Helmets were optional for college players until 1939. The NFL didn't require them until 1943. If a player did wear a helmet, it was usually made of leather. The first plastic helmet was invented in 1939 by sporting goods manufacturer Riddell. But because of a plastics shortage due to World War II (1939–45), the NFL outlawed plastic helmets until 1949. The facemask came along in 1955.

A WORK OF ART

Football helmets usually feature iconic logos that identify the team immediately. But early helmets were plain. The first design appeared in 1948 when Los Angeles Rams halfback Fred Gehrke painted horns on the team's helmets.

Shoulder pads have been a part of the football uniform for much longer. They date back to 1877, when they were sewn into the jersey. It wasn't until the early 1900s that shoulder pads became a separate piece of equipment. They were made of leather, wool, and canvas until the 1960s, when plastic took over. By the 1980s, shoulder pads had become bulky. Today's pads are much smaller. Thanks to

Cleveland Browns quarterback Otto Graham was the first player to wear a facemask in an NFL game. He taped a plastic bar to his helmet after being elbowed during a game.

Shoulder pads are made from a plastic outer shell that covers a material designed to absorb shock.

higher quality materials and efficient design, modern pads offer better protection, more mobility, and more comfort.

Football shoes have also undergone big changes. In the game's early years, players' shoes did not have cleats. Then players added their own cleats. Now, football shoes come with cleats that are made for all sorts of different conditions, such as muddy fields or artificial turf.

In the NFL, jersey numbers are dictated by a player's primary position. Only certain players are allowed to catch the ball or run downfield before a pass. Having distinct number ranges for different positions helps officials spot these players. For example, quarterbacks can wear Nos. 0 through 19 only. Running backs, receivers, and tight ends are assigned jersey numbers between 0 and 49 or between 80 and 89.

The football itself has changed over time, too. It was much more rounded at the sport's beginning. As the ball became more oblong and streamlined, it helped make the forward pass easier. Now the size of the football varies depending on the age group or level of play.

CHAPTER SEVEN

OTHER FORMS OF FOOTBALL

KURT WARNER'S JOURNEY

There's no guaranteed path to football stardom. Quarterback Kurt Warner was cut after his first NFL training camp. He got a job at a grocery store while working to stay in shape. Eventually he landed a job with an Arena Football League team. After three record-setting years, he signed with the St. Louis Rams. Over 12 NFL seasons with the Rams, New York Giants, and Arizona Cardinals, Warner won two MVP awards and one Super Bowl. He was later inducted into the Pro Football Hall of Fame.

A football team has 11 players on the field at a time, and a football field is 100 yards long. Except when it isn't. The CFL field looks a lot like the one used in the NFL. But there are also some key differences. The CFL field is longer and wider. Midfield is the 55-yard line instead of the 50. The end zones are 20 yards deep instead of 10. Goal posts are at the front of the end zone, with the crossbar directly

Until 1986, CFL end zones were 25 yards deep. That year they were shortened to 20 yards.

Small towns such as Simla (in blue) and Elbert, Colorado compete in 8-man football. Simla has a population of 601 people. Only 188 people live in Elbert.

above the goal line. The NFL moved goal posts to the back of the end zone in 1974.

Instead of having four downs to gain 10 yards, CFL offenses get only three downs. Each team has 12 players on the field, not 11. There's a slight difference in scoring, too. The kicking team can score one point, called a "rouge," if the opposing team fails to return the ball out of the end zone on a missed field goal or on a punt.

Arena football teams have fewer players on the field than in NFL games. The field is only 50 yards long. Only eight players per side are allowed. That's just one of many differences to make the game work on a smaller field. There is also no punting, so teams must either go for a first down or a field goal on fourth down. Goal posts are narrower than in the outdoor game. In addition, in arena football, nets on the outside of the goal posts allow the opposing team a chance to return missed field goals.

Sometimes traditional football games use fewer than 11 players per side. This is most often found at the high school level, when smaller communities don't have enough players to field 11 at a time. In these other versions, the width of the field is usually cut from the standard 53 1/3 yards to 40 yards. The length is often shortened from 100 yards to 80. The most common small-school variants are

9-man, 8-man, and 6-man football. Other rule changes for small-sided games include how many players have to start on the line of scrimmage and who is eligible to catch a pass.

Tackling is a fundamental skill in football. But many kids learn to play in a version of the sport without tackling. This is called flag football. In this version of the game, players wear belts with flags attached to each hip. A player is considered down when their flag or flag belt is removed. The field is usually smaller, and the teams feature anywhere from five to 10 players per side.

In recent years, flag football has grown in popularity. More people are playing the sport at older levels, since it is less intense and aggressive than traditional football. The sport is also easier to play because it requires less equipment. This has helped make it appealing to people who don't have as many opportunities to play the sport, including girls and those outside of North America. Flag football got a major boost when it was added to the 2028 Olympics.

High school players demonstrated flag football at Philadelphia's Lincoln Financial Field during halftime of a 2023 preseason NFL game between the Philadelphia Eagles and the Indianapolis Colts.

CHAPTER EIGHT

WOMEN IN FOOTBALL

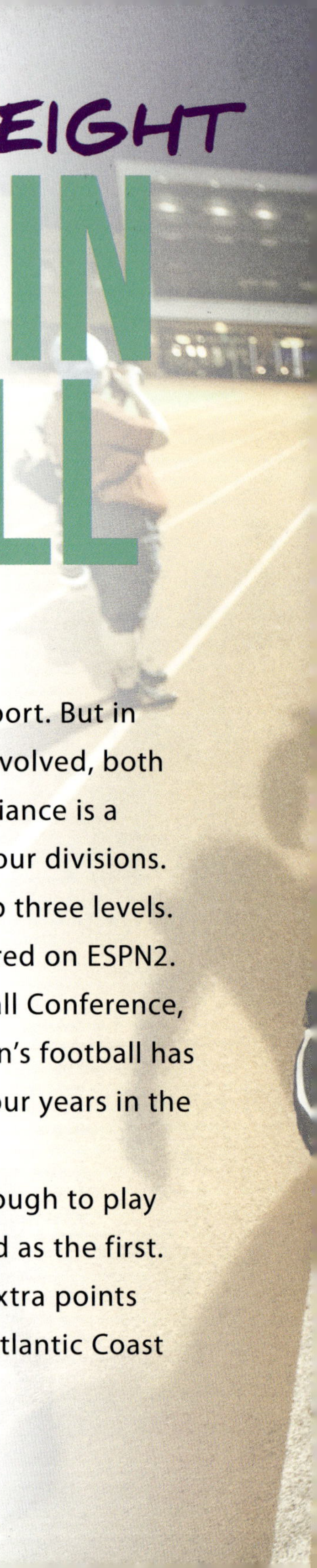

Football is traditionally a male-dominated sport. But in recent years, women are becoming more involved, both on the field and off. The Women's Football Alliance is a tackle football league formed in 2009. It has four divisions. As of 2023, there were 55 teams across the top three levels. The league's championship game has been aired on ESPN2. Another league, the Women's National Football Conference, began in 2019. It had 16 teams in 2023. Women's football has national teams as well. They compete every four years in the Senior Women's World Championship.

In addition, some women have broken through to play on men's teams. Patricia Palinkas is recognized as the first. In 1970, she held the ball for field goals and extra points as a member of the Orlando Panthers of the Atlantic Coast

Linebacker Melisa Cadet and the Boston Renegades won their fourth straight Women's Football Alliance championship in 2023.

Ashley Martin (89) played on the Jacksonville State football team for one season. She also played soccer at the school.

Football League. Several women have followed by playing in college games. Most of them were kickers.

Liz Heaston was the first. She played for Willamette University, a lower-level team, in 1997. Ashley Martin kicked an extra point for Jacksonville State in 2001. That made her the first woman to score at the NCAA level. Katie Hnida was the first to score in an FBS game, doing so for New Mexico in 2003. In 2023, safety Haley Van Voorhis of Shenandoah University made history as the first woman to play at a position other than kicker in an NCAA game.

Women have also broken through on the field as officials. Sarah Thomas became the first female official in NFL history in 2015. In 2023, three women officiated in the NFL with many more working toward joining them. Even more

WOMEN BROADCASTING FOOTBALL

Women have been a part of NFL broadcasts since 1974, when CBS hired Jane Chastain as an in-game analyst. A year later Phyllis George was hired to co-host CBS's weekly NFL pregame show. Many women have since followed. In 1987, Gayle Sierens became the first female play-by-play announcer for an NFL game on TV. It took another 30 years before Beth Mowins became the next woman to call an NFL game. She handled a *Monday Night Football* broadcast on ESPN in 2017. Pam Ward became the first woman to do play-by-play for ESPN on a college broadcast in 2000.

women officiate at the college level. In 2023, the Hula Bowl had an all-female officiating crew.

Women have also made gains in other roles. In 1997, Amy Trask became the NFL's first female chief executive when the Oakland Raiders hired her. She began as an intern in 1987 in the Raiders' legal department and worked her way up to the top of the organization. Twelve women have owned NFL franchises as of 2023. Meanwhile, Kathryn Smith became the first woman with a full-time coaching position in the NFL. She was hired as the Buffalo Bills' special teams quality control coach in 2016.

Kathryn Smith spent one season as a special teams coach for the Buffalo Bills.

CHAPTER NINE

BIG MOMENTS, BIG PLAYS

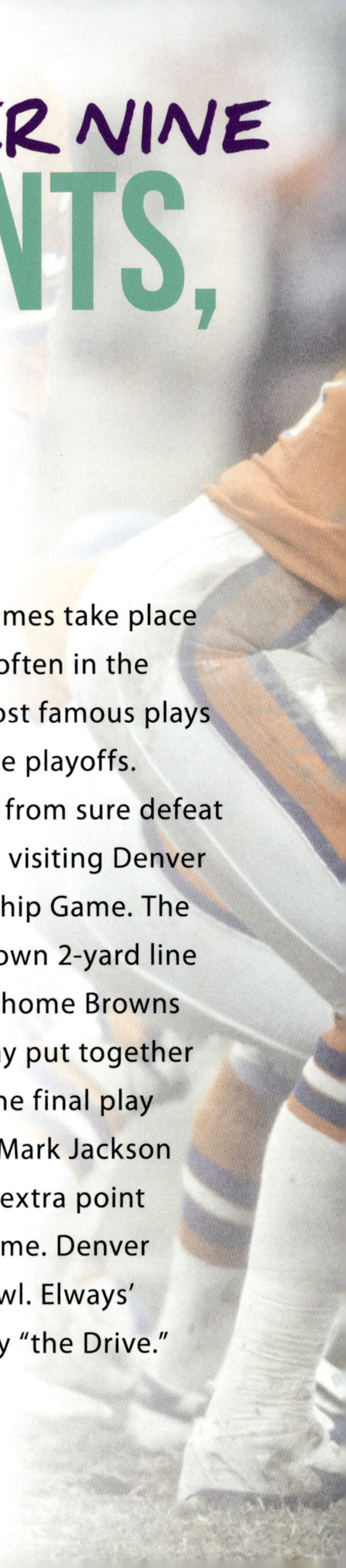

The biggest plays and most memorable games take place on the biggest stages. In the NFL, that is often in the playoffs. It's no surprise that many of the most famous plays and games in league history happened in the playoffs.

Miraculous comebacks have taken teams from sure defeat to shocking victory. On January 11, 1987, the visiting Denver Broncos trailed 20–13 in the AFC Championship Game. The Cleveland Browns had Denver pinned at its own 2-yard line with just over five minutes to play. With the home Browns fans roaring, Broncos quarterback John Elway put together a 15-play drive. Denver marched 98 yards. The final play was a five-yard touchdown pass to receiver Mark Jackson with 39 seconds left in regulation. After the extra point tied the game, the two teams went to overtime. Denver eventually won 23–20 to go to the Super Bowl. Elways' heroics have since been referred to as simply "the Drive."

Denver Broncos quarterback John Elway (7) shouts signals while taking on the Cleveland Browns in the AFC Championship Game on January 11, 1987.

THE PLAY

College football fans know exactly what "the Play" refers to. It involves a band, two football teams, and a crazy ending to a game. In 1982, Stanford took a 20–19 lead over California with four seconds left. On the kickoff, California made several laterals to keep the ball alive. Somehow, the Golden Bears' Kevin Moen ended up with the ball and a clear path to the end zone. Well, not *completely* clear. He had to dodge members of the Stanford band, who thought that the game was over and had spilled out onto the field. Moen scored the touchdown, flattening a trombone player in the process, and California got the victory.

On January 8, 2000, the Tennessee Titans pulled off the "Music City Miracle." The Buffalo Bills took a 16–15 lead with 16 seconds left in an AFC wild-card game at Tennessee. On the following kickoff, Titans running back Lorenzo Neal fielded the ball and handed it to tight end Frank Wycheck. The Bills didn't see wide receiver Kevin Dyson on the opposite sideline. Wycheck threw the ball backward and across the field to Dyson. Before the Bills could react, Dyson took off. No defender got near him as he ran 75 yards for the game-winning touchdown.

The "Minneapolis Miracle" happened on January 14, 2018. The Minnesota Vikings trailed the New Orleans Saints 24–23 with 10 seconds left in their NFC playoff game. From his own 30-yard line, Vikings quarterback Case Keenum threw a pass that wide receiver Stefon Diggs caught on the sideline.

The "Music City Miracle" helped propel the Tennessee Titans to the Super Bowl in January 2000.

Two New Orleans Saints defenders were right next to Diggs. But both missed tackling the Vikings receiver. Instead, they collided. Diggs turned to see a clear path to the end zone. He sprinted the last 30 yards for the winning score.

The largest comeback in Super Bowl history happened in Super Bowl LI on February 5, 2017. The Atlanta Falcons led the New England Patriots 28–3 in the third quarter. But Tom Brady and the Patriots came all the way back to tie it, then running back James White scored in overtime to win 34–28.

The largest comeback in NFL playoff history happened on January 3, 1993. On a frigid day in Buffalo, the Bills trailed by 32 points in the third quarter of an AFC wild-card game against the Houston Oilers. Even worse, Buffalo's starting quarterback, Jim Kelly, was injured during the first half. Kelly's backup, Frank Reich, rallied the team with four touchdown passes. Buffalo stormed back with five straight touchdowns to take a 38–35 lead. The stunned Oilers recovered to kick a game-tying field goal. But the Bills won in overtime when kicker Steve Christie knocked in a 32-yard field goal of his own to cap an incredible 41–38 win.

Some big catches have become famous, too. One was so iconic, it's called "the Catch." Late in the 1981 NFC Championship Game, 49ers quarterback Joe Montana heaved a pass toward the back of the end zone.

Minnesota Vikings receiver Stefon Diggs celebrates as he crosses the goal line to complete the "Minneapolis Miracle" in January 2018.

Receiver Dwight Clark made a leaping, fingertip catch to beat the Dallas Cowboys. Late in Super Bowl XLII after the 2007 season, the New York Giants' David Tyree caught a long pass by pinning the ball against his helmet as he fell to the ground. It helped the Giants upset the previously undefeated Patriots and became known as the "Helmet Catch."

In the 1972 playoffs, the "Immaculate Reception" shocked the NFL. Pittsburgh Steelers quarterback Terry Bradshaw threw a last-gasp pass against the Oakland Raiders. The ball bounced off an Oakland defender and went flying back toward the line of scrimmage. It looked like it would fall incomplete. Then, Pittsburgh running back Franco Harris swooped in and grabbed the ball just before it hit the ground. He then raced down the sideline for the winning touchdown.

THE KICK SIX

The University of Alabama entered its 2013 game against archrival Auburn 11–0 and ranked No. 1 in the country. With one second left in a 28–28 tie, Alabama kicker Adam Griffith lined up a potential game-winning 57-yard field goal. Griffith's attempt came up short and was caught by Auburn's Chris Davis in the end zone. In front of the screaming Auburn fans, Davis ran the ball back 109 yards for an incredible game-winning score. Many observers consider the play to be the greatest finish in college football history.

Few NFL fans knew who David Tyree was before his famous "Helmet Catch" in Super Bowl XLII. The play made him an instant legend.

CHAPTER TEN

FANTASY FOOTBALL

Every week during the NFL season, millions of people from around the world put their own football lineups together in the hopes of winning a game. They don't own a real football team. They're just playing fantasy football.

Fantasy football teams earn points based on the statistics of real-life players. But one owner's fantasy team will include players from many NFL teams. That gives fantasy football owners a reason to pay attention to the whole league.

Though fantasy football traces its roots to the 1960s, its popularity soared in the 1990s. Before then, fantasy owners usually had to wait until they got their newspaper on Monday morning to find out how their players did. That all changed when more and more Americans gained regular access to the internet.

Fantasy football players often gather to hold their player drafts before the season starts.

Sports websites began providing live updates of NFL games. They soon started leagues and updating fantasy scores in real time. Other sites sprang up, offering advice on which players to start each week. Eventually, daily fantasy providers offered the chance to pick a whole new team every week.

FANTASY PIONEERS

The first known fantasy football league was formed in 1962. Bill Winkenbach, part owner of the Oakland Raiders, and a few of his friends came up with the concept. Their first draft was held at a hotel in New York City. They called it the GOPPPL, short for the Greater Oakland Professional Pigskin Prognosticators League.

An estimated 3 million people in the United States and Canada played fantasy football in 1994. By 2015, that number had grown to 40 million. It's also been a huge financial success. Exact totals are hard to pin down, but the global fantasy football market was estimated between $18 billion and $22 billion in 2021.

Fantasy football has changed the viewing experience even for people who don't play. Broadcasters often cite fantasy statistics during NFL games. Pregame shows are filled with fantasy advice. And the concept of fantasy sports has spread to baseball, basketball, soccer, and more—if it's a sport, there's probably a fantasy version of it available.

Minnesota Vikings running back Adrian Peterson was named the NFL's Fantasy Player of the Year in 2012.

GLOSSARY

cleats

Spikes built into the sole of a shoe to aid the wearer's traction.

contract

An agreement to play for a certain team.

dynasties

Teams that have extended periods of success, usually winning multiple championships in the process.

efficient

Productive and without wasted effort.

evolve

Develop over time.

gimmick

A trick or skill that a person uses to attract attention.

iconic

Well known for excellence.

intern

Someone who does a certain job to gain experience, often without being paid.

line of scrimmage

The place on the field where a play starts.

merge

Join with another to create something new, such as a company, a team, or a league.

modern

Current or present.

professional

A person who gets paid to perform.

rival

An opponent with whom a player or team has a fierce and ongoing competition.

MORE INFORMATION

Books

Graves, Will. *GOATs of Football*. Abdo Publishing, 2022.

Hanlon, Luke. *Football Strategies*. Abdo Publishing, 2024.

Holloway, Jerrett and Rafael Thomas. *Football: A Beginner's Guide*. Rockridge Press, 2022.

Online Resources

Booklinks
NONFICTION NETWORK
FREE! ONLINE NONFICTION RESOURCES

To learn more about football, please visit **abdobooklinks.com** or scan this QR code. These links are routinely monitored and updated to provide the most current information available.

INDEX

About the Author

Corbu Stathes lives in Minnesota with his son. He works in college sports and loves researching and learning about new things.